D1273888

OUR BODY

Muscular System

Cheryl Jakab

Smart Apple Media

This edition first published in 2006 in the United States of America by Smart Apple Media.

Smart Apple Media
2140 Howard Drive West
North Mankato
Minnesota 56003

First published in 2006 by
MACMILLAN EDUCATION AUSTRALIA PTY LTD
627 Chapel Street, South Yarra, Australia 3141

Visit our Web site at www.macmillan.com.au

Associated companies and representatives throughout the world.

Library of Congress Cataloging-in-Publication Data

Jakab, Cheryl.
    The muscular system / by Cheryl Jakab.
    p. cm. — (Our body)
    Includes index.
    ISBN-13: 978-1-58340-734-9
    1. Musculoskeletal system—Juvenile literature. I. Title.

QP301.J35 2006
612.7—dc22   2005056804

Edited by Ruth Jelley
Text and cover design by Peter Shaw
Illustrations by Guy Holt, Jeff Lang (p. 4 (bottom), pp. 5–6),
    and Ann Likhovetsky (p. 30)
Photo research by Legend Images

Printed in USA

Acknowledgments
The author and the publisher are grateful to the following for permission to reproduce copyright material:

Front cover photograph: Colored SEM/scanning electron micrograph of freeze-fractured skeletal muscle fiber, courtesy of Photolibrary/Steve Gschmeissner/Science Photo Library. Front cover illustration by Jeff Lang.

Sercomi-B.S.I.P./Auscape International, p. 16; Bill Thomas/Imagen, p. 28; Photodisc, pp. 18, 19, 21, 22, 23; Photolibrary/Science Photo Library, pp. 9, 10, 17, 26.

While every care has been taken to trace and acknowledge copyright, the publisher tenders their apologies for any accidental infringement where copyright has proved untraceable. Where the attempt has been unsuccessful, the publisher welcomes information that would redress the situation.

Contents

Glossary words
When a word is printed in **bold**, you can look up its meaning in the Glossary on page 31.

Amazing body structures

The human body is an amazing living thing. The structures of the body are divided into systems. Each system is made up of **cells**. Huge numbers of cells make up the **tissues** of the body systems. Each system performs a different, vital function. This series looks at six of the systems in the most familiar living thing to you–your body.

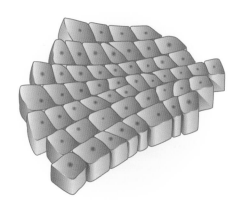

Cells make up tissues of the body systems.

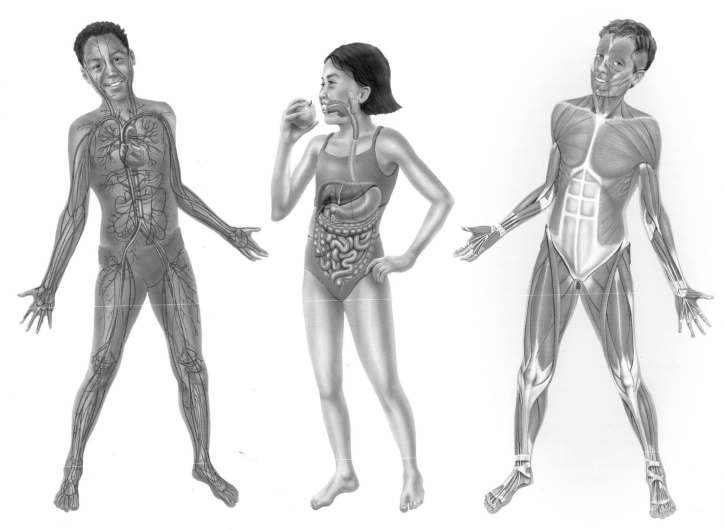

circulatory system   digestive system   muscular system

The muscular system

The muscular system moves all of your body parts. How much do you know about your muscular system?

- How many muscles do you have?
- What does each muscle do in your body?
- How do your muscles change as you grow?
- What happens if you tear a muscle?

This book looks at the human muscular system to answer these questions and more.

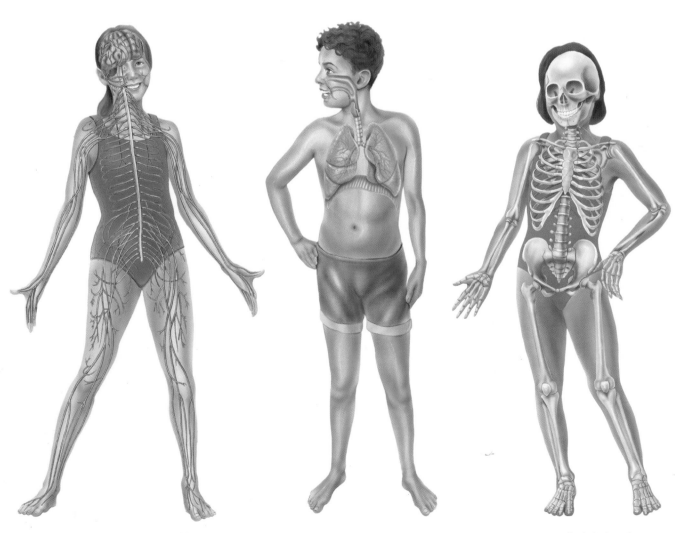

nervous system

respiratory system

skeletal system

Parts of the muscular system

The muscular system is made up of all the **skeletal muscles** in the body. Skeletal muscles are voluntary muscles, which are controlled by deliberate actions. When we want to move part of our body, a nerve signal is sent from the brain to the muscle, which makes it **contract**.

Other types of muscle in the body, cardiac muscle and smooth muscle, are not part of the muscular system. These muscles are different from skeletal muscles because they are involuntary muscles, which are automatically controlled by the nervous system. They work constantly without you having to think about them. Cardiac and smooth muscles are also made up of different types of **muscle fiber** to skeletal muscles.

FASCINATING FACT

The muscular system is the largest part of the human body. It makes up about half of the body's total weight.

nasalis

trapezius

zygomaticus major

deltoid

pectoralis major

rectus abdominus

biceps brachii

triceps

quadriceps femoris

tibialis anterior

gastrocnemius

Skeletal muscles are used to move the body.

Skeletal muscles

Skeletal muscles attach to the bones of the skeleton. Most skeletal muscles attach to one bone and stretch across a joint to attach to another bone. There are about 640 muscles that work together to move the various parts of the body.

Superficial and deep muscles

The muscular system is made up of two overlapping layers of muscles, called superficial and deep muscles. Superficial muscles are located on the surface, just under the skin. Deep muscles form a layer beneath the superficial muscles.

TRY THIS

See for yourself

Get a joint of meat, such as a shoulder of lamb, from the butcher. Carefully take the joint apart to see bundles of muscle fibers. Look for the places where the muscles attach to the bones.

deep muscles

superficial muscles

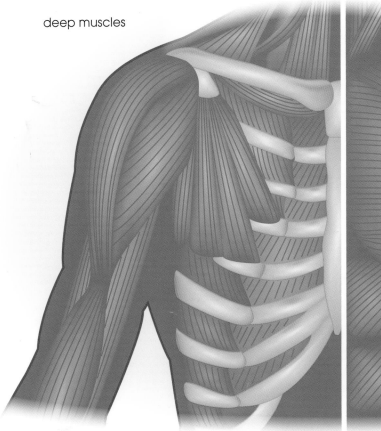
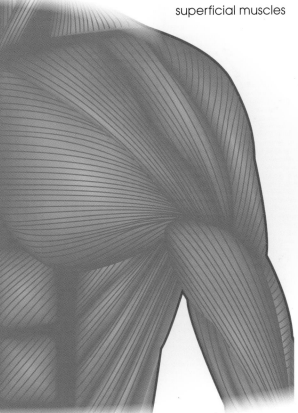

Muscles give the body its shape.

Front and back muscles

The muscles on the front and back of the body have different patterns. The front of the body has three layers of **abdominal** muscles, each running in a different direction. These layers form a strong wall over the stomach area where there are no bones covering internal organs. On the back of the body, the muscles attach to the spine and form a massive triangle.

FASCINATING FACT

The largest muscle in the body is the gluteus maximus in the buttocks, which is involved in leg movements. The smallest muscle in the body, the stapedius, is in the ear. It contracts to protect the ear from very loud sounds.

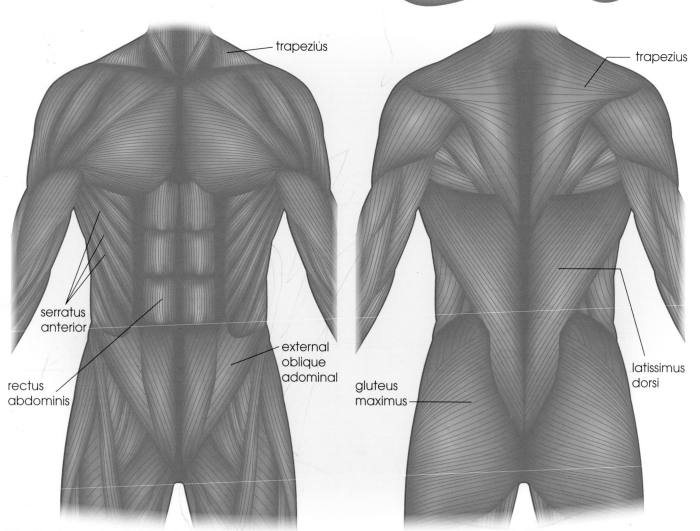

trapezius

trapezius

serratus anterior

external oblique adominal

rectus abdominis

gluteus maximus

latissimus dorsi

The front muscles (left) help protect internal organs, while the back muscles (right) help hold the spine upright.

Muscle fibers

Muscles are made up of long, string-like fibers which run parallel to each other. They occur in bundles with a covering around them, called a **sheath**. Each fiber is thinner than a human hair and very long. One muscle fiber can be up to 12 inches (30 cm) long. Muscle fibers change in length by contracting and relaxing. Contracting shortens muscle fibers. The fibers are at their longest when the muscle is relaxed.

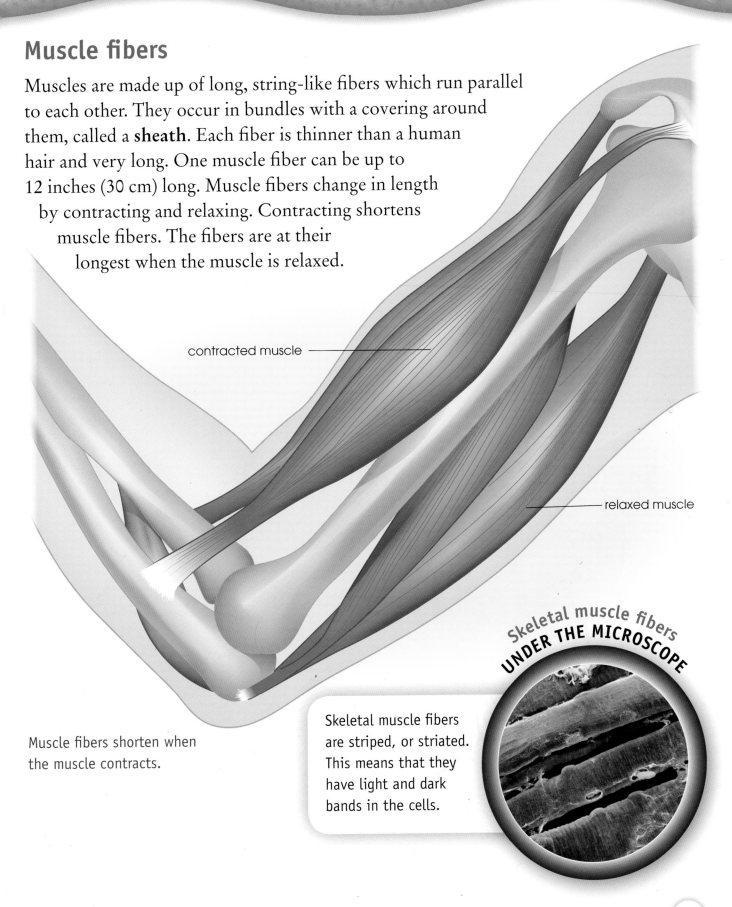

contracted muscle

relaxed muscle

Muscle fibers shorten when the muscle contracts.

Skeletal muscle fibers are striped, or striated. This means that they have light and dark bands in the cells.

Skeletal muscle fibers
UNDER THE MICROSCOPE

Tendons

Tendons link muscles to bones. They are strong bands of connecting tissue which form from the ends of the muscle sheath. The end of the tendon passes through the outer covering of bone (the periosteum) to firmly anchor inside the bone.

Tendons can be long or short. Hands have very long tendons which connect the fingers to the muscles in the forearm that control them.

The outer sheath of some tendons, such as in those in the knee, produce a **lubricant**. This lubricant protects the tendons where they rub against bones during movement.

**Tendon fibres
UNDER THE MICROSCOPE**

Tendon fibers are made of a strong stringy material called collagen. They are much stronger than muscle fibers.

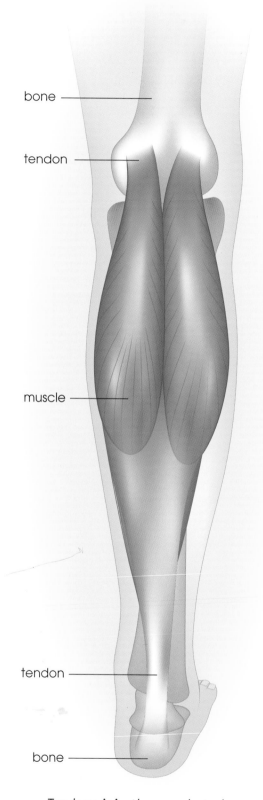

bone

tendon

muscle

tendon

bone

Tendons join the muscle to bone above the knee and in the heel.

peroneus longus

tibialis anterior

gastrocnemius

achilles tendon

The muscles in the lower leg control
the movement of the foot.

Leg and foot muscles

Leg and foot muscles work together in
activities such as walking, running, cycling,
and dancing. Strong tendons attach these
muscles across the joints of the hip, knee,
ankle, and toes.

The large, powerful **thigh** muscles
surround the largest bone in the body, the
femur. These muscles **originate** in the hip
and join the femur just above the knee.
The calf muscle (gastrocnemius) in the
lower leg is smaller than the thigh muscles
but still very powerful. The gastrocnemius
originates above the knee at the back of
the femur and joins the bone at the heel.
The muscles in the front of the lower leg
have very long tendons which connect to
the toes.

FASCINATING FACT

The Achilles tendon attaches the
gastrocnemius to the heel. It is
named after the Ancient Greek hero,
Achilles, whose one weakness was
in his heel. In the ancient story,
Achilles was killed by an arrow
shot into his heel.

The shoulder

The shoulder is controlled by a team of muscles which surround the joint. It is the most **flexible** of all the joints in the body and can be moved in full circles. The deltoid muscle wraps over the shoulder to firmly hold the joint in place.

Arm and hand muscles

The muscles in the hand and lower arm control the hand, giving it a wide range of movement. The muscles of the lower arm are connected to the fingers by very long tendons which run down the forearm to the fingertips. This allows the hands to be small while being very strong. If the forearm muscles themselves were in the hand then the fingers would be very thick. They would be unable to perform fine and precise movements, such as writing.

deltoid

pectoralis major

brachioradialis

Long muscles in the forearm control the tendons in the hand.

thenar muscles

tendons

Facial muscles

Facial muscles contract to produce facial expressions such as smiling, frowning, looking sad, and laughing. There are about 30 muscles that change the shape of the face. Facial muscles are attached at one end to the skull bones. The other ends of the muscles are attached to the skin, not bones. So when facial muscles contract, they pull the skin into different shapes.

Facial expressions

Each facial expression is made using a range of muscles. Very small changes in the shape of the face can express different feelings. Contracting the zygomaticus muscles, for instance, creates a smile by lifting the corners of the mouth. It is easier to smile than frown because it takes about half as many muscles.

TRY THIS

Flare your nostrils

Try flaring your nostrils wide. You can do this by contracting the levator labii superioris muscles strongly. Practicing flaring the nostrils can help strengthen these muscles.

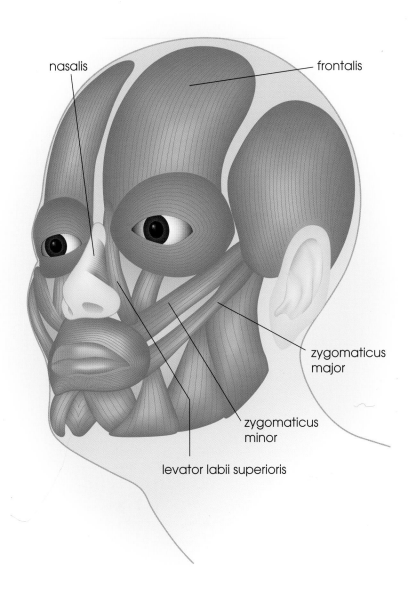

nasalis

frontalis

zygomaticus major

zygomaticus minor

levator labii superioris

There are many muscles in the face which are used to create facial expressions.

Contraction

Contracting a muscle moves the bones or skin the muscle is attached to. For example, contracting the biceps muscle causes the arm to bend at the elbow. Most of the muscles in the body work in this way.

Contraction of the biceps muscle causes the elbow to bend.

Pulling force

When a muscle contracts it applies a pulling force which pulls the bone. The pulling force is applied at the point where the tendon joins the bone. Contracting the biceps muscle pulls the bones in the forearm, the radius, and ulna, towards the shoulder. This movement causes the elbow joint to bend. The origin of a muscle stays in a fixed position as the muscle contracts. The origin of the biceps muscle is attached to the shoulder, which remains still as the arm bends.

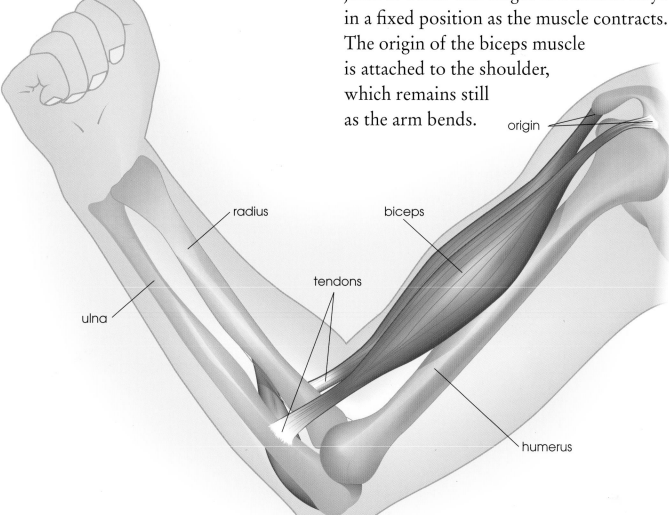

origin

radius

biceps

tendons

ulna

humerus

Bending and straightening

The biceps muscle contracts to bend the arm, but it cannot push to straighten the arm again. Another muscle, the triceps, must contract to straighten the arm. The biceps muscle relaxes as the triceps muscle contracts, so it does not fight the movement of the arm. When the biceps muscle contracts, the triceps muscle relaxes.

Muscle pairs

The biceps and triceps muscles work as a pair to move the forearm. Any two muscles that work together as a pair are called **antagonists**. Their actions are opposite to each other. When one contracts, the other relaxes. Muscles all over the body work in this way to coordinate all of the body's movements.

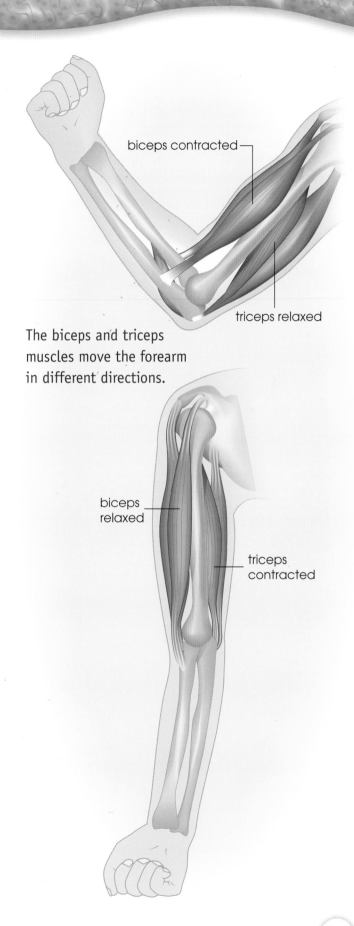

biceps contracted

triceps relaxed

The biceps and triceps muscles move the forearm in different directions.

biceps relaxed

triceps contracted

TRY THIS

Find muscle pairs

Find a muscle pair by placing your hands on the front and back of your lower leg. Point your foot down to feel the gastrocnemius contract. Which muscle contracts when you lift your toes back up toward your knee?

How muscles contract

When a muscle gets the signal to contract, each long fiber within the muscle shortens. There are **filaments** within the muscle fibers that slide over each other when a muscle contracts. This makes each fiber shorter so the overall muscle is shorter.

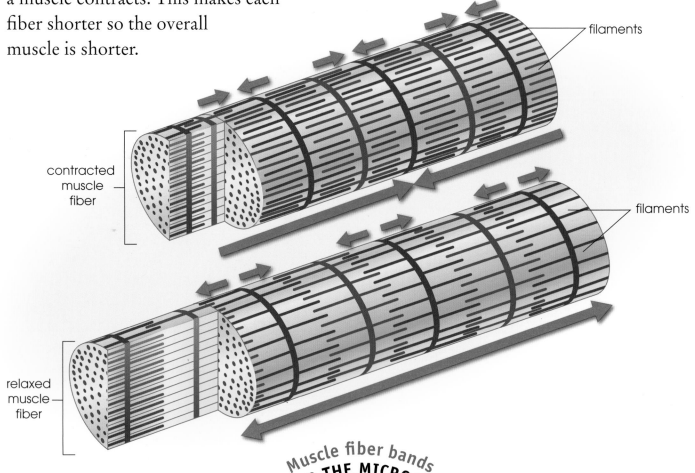

filaments

contracted muscle fiber

filaments

relaxed muscle fiber

Filaments slide over each other to shorten the muscle when it contracts.

Muscle fiber bands
UNDER THE MICROSCOPE

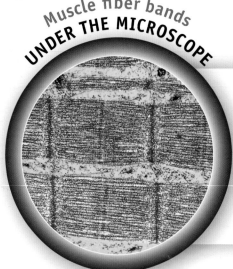

There are bands, or striations, within muscle fibers. Contraction occurs within these bands. A microscope shows the striations in the fibers are closer together when a muscle is contracted.

Energy for muscles

Muscles need **energy** to contract. The action of filaments sliding over each other uses up energy and produces **waste**. Muscles use a form of energy called glucose, which is carried to the muscle in the bloodstream. Wastes produced in the muscles are also carried away in the blood. The body creates glucose from the food that is eaten.

Muscle heat and sweat

When muscles work hard they produce heat, which causes the skin to produce sweat. Sweating is the body's way of keeping muscles cool.

A thermogram, or heat picture, shows the amount of heat that is produced by the body. The different colors show that varying amounts of heat are produced in different areas. White indicates areas that are producing the most heat, followed by red, yellow, green, blue, and purple. Black areas are those which produce the least amount of heat.

FASCINATING FACT

Oxygen is needed for the muscles to burn glucose. When you exercise, breathing increases in order to deliver the extra oxygen that is needed by the muscles.

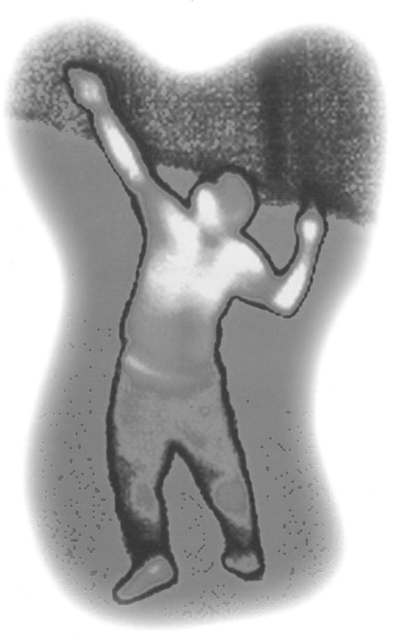

A thermogram shows this tennis player is losing the most heat through the abdomen, head, chest, and arms.

Controlling movement

Very young babies have little **muscle tone** and cannot control their movements. Skillful movements, such as walking and writing, are developed over many years. Although everybody develops slightly differently, there is a general pattern of muscle development that babies go through.

Hand and arm muscles

As hand and arm muscles develop, a child's skill in holding and moving objects increases. At around six months old babies can pass objects from one hand to the other. After about 18 months they can hold a crayon and scribble. By the time they are three years old, control of their hand muscles allows them to copy lines and draw within shapes. By the age of four years, children can copy letters and draw figures. Most five-year-old children can copy shapes and write letters. These precise movements require a great deal of fine control over the muscles in the arms and hands.

FASCINATING FACT
Newborn babies automatically grasp objects that are put into their hands. This is known as a reflex action. It is thought that babies develop this reflex to help them hold on to their mothers.

Good control of the hand and arm muscles is necessary for writing and drawing.

Developing major muscles

Muscles that are used for sitting, crawling, walking, and running develop tone gradually over the first two years of a child's life. Newborn babies do not have strong neck muscles and cannot hold up their heads. At one month old, most babies still lie on their backs with their head to the side. By the age of three years most children can run with ease and kick a ball. This may take longer for some toddlers, while others develop these skills earlier. Skill in moving the body increases with repeated practice. Whether it is playing the piano, tap dancing, or kicking a soccer ball, strength and control of muscles is developed through practice. Repetition builds muscle strength and allows actions to be performed without having to think about them.

Strong neck and shoulder muscles are needed to hold up the head and chest.

FASCINATING FACT
Even thinking about practicing actions can help improve muscular skills. Many sports coaches find mental rehearsal (going over the actions in the mind) assists in refining motor skills.

Muscles and posture

All the muscles in the **torso** and **limbs** remain partially contracted to maintain **posture**. They must be strong enough to hold the body upright. The powerful muscles of the back hold the spine in the correct position while sitting and standing. These muscles also provide strength for lifting and pushing movements.

Sitting up straight and standing tall help strengthen the smaller deep muscles along the spine. When sitting still or working on the computer for a long time, many muscles are constantly contracted and need a rest. Doing something different, such as standing or walking, will help to rest those muscles.

HEALTH TIP
Exercise

Exercising all the muscles in the body is necessary for overall fitness. Slow, controlled movements using all the different muscles of the body help develop overall muscle tone.

Tip: Exercise programs such as Tai Chi are ideal for developing overall muscle tone.

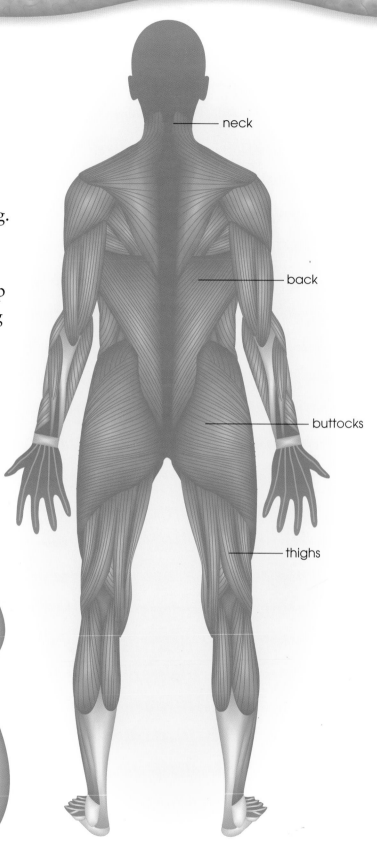

neck

back

buttocks

thighs

Large muscles in the neck, back, buttocks, and thighs are used to hold the body upright.

Muscular differences

Boys and girls have very similar muscular development before **puberty**. As they mature, however, the pattern of muscle development is different in males and females. Adult males generally have broader shoulders with stronger arm and chest muscles than females. Men are stronger in the upper body than women, compared to their overall body size.

FASCINATING FACT

Weight-lifting is an Olympic sport that is designed to test muscle strength. The weight-lifters are classed according to body size, the smallest being the 121 pound (55 kg) class. The heaviest weight lifted at the Athens Olympics in 2004 was 589 pounds (267 kg).

Males develop stronger muscles than females after **puberty**.

Healthy muscles

Muscles that are regularly worked hard become strong and healthy. Exercise builds up muscle tissue and makes each fiber stronger. In the past, most people got a great deal of exercise each day which helped keep their muscles healthy. People used to walk everywhere, whereas now we use faster forms of transportation, such as cars and trains. Many people today spend much of their time sitting at a desk or a computer for work and entertainment. This sort of lifestyle leads to loss of strength and tone in muscles.

HEALTH TIP
Energy for exercise

Athletes can load up on energy by eating high carbohydrate foods. The energy is stored as a complex sugar known as glycogen, which is converted to glucose when the muscles work.

Tip: Eat high carbohydrate foods two days before a hard workout.

Exercise programs

Exercise programs should give every muscle a workout. Swimming is one type of exercise that involves all the muscles of the body and is gentle on joints. The water also helps cool the muscles as they work.

Swimming helps to build muscle strength by exercising all the muscles in the body.

Maintaining muscle tone

Constant contraction of the back and neck muscles maintains muscle tone. These muscles remain contracted even when we are not moving, in order to hold up the head and keep the spine upright. The brain constantly sends messages to these muscles to keep them contracted. Maintaining good posture helps to keep these muscles strong so that they can hold the body in the correct position.

Flexibility

Muscles and tendons need to be flexible as well as strong. Stretching exercises can help maintain and improve flexibility. This is particularly important for tendons and muscles that are not used very often.

A lacrosse player stretches his legs before a game.

Muscles during sleep

Most muscles relax during sleep, but some of them remain contracted. If you watch somebody fall asleep you can see their muscles slowly relax.

FASCINATING FACT

Gymnasts develop strong arm and hand muscles to hold their whole body weight for doing handstands. Eventually they develop automatic balance in handstands, just as most people do for standing on their feet.

Muscular problems

Muscles do not suffer from many diseases. However, muscle strains or tears can occur during strenuous exercise or in an accident. If one part of a muscle is damaged another part can grow larger and stronger to replace the damaged fibers.

Muscle strain

Damage to muscle fibres is called a muscle strain. This can cause bleeding, soreness, swelling, and bruising in the affected muscle. If the damage involves a large number of muscle fibers the injury is called a muscle tear.

deltoid

tear

humerus

Muscular dystrophy

Muscular dystrophy is a set of muscle diseases that cause skeletal muscles to shrink and waste away. Sufferers eventually lose the ability to use their muscles. There is no known treatment, but stretching exercises and surgery can help some sufferers. Scientists continue to research and find out more about the condition.

A muscle can tear during exercise, particularly if the body is not properly prepared.

Poliomyelitis

Poliomyelitis (polio) is a nerve disease that leads to loss of muscle in the affected parts of the body. This disease was once common but was brought under control in the 1940s.

Tendon problems

Tendons, and the sheath around them, can suffer from a number of problems.

Tendonitis

Tendonitis, the swelling of tendons, occurs when tendons rub against bones. Tennis and squash players often experience pain in the shoulder due to the rubbing of the supraspinous tendon on the shoulder blade bone. The swelling increases the rubbing of the tendon, so rest is needed to allow the tendon to return to normal. Walking in poorly fitted shoes can cause the large tendon sheath at the front of the foot to swell.

Tendon tears

A sudden and strong muscle contraction can cause a tendon to tear away from the bone. The extensor tendon on the top of the finger can tear if an object, such as a ball, hits the tip of the finger. Sometimes tendons in the ankle are torn when the ankle is twisted.

FASCINATING FACT

Repetitive Strain Injury (RSI) occurs in people who repeat finger actions continuously, such as piano players and keyboard users. RSI causes swelling of the tendons in the wrist, which leads to severe pain when the fingers are moved.

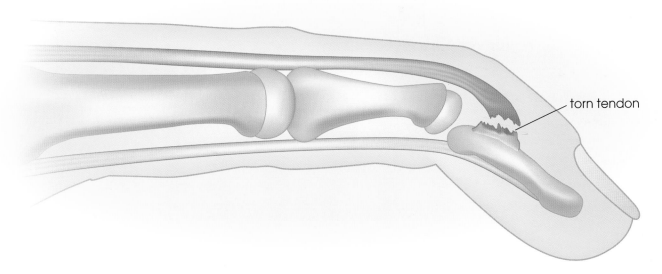

torn tendon

A torn finger tendon can take several months to heal.

Treating problems

Physical therapists treat muscle and tendon problems. Physical therapy can help with muscle and tendon damage and postural problems.

Relearning to use muscles

After an accident or a long period of bed rest, patients often have to learn how to use their muscles again. Physical therapy can help people relearn to use their muscles in a way that best suits their needs.

Muscle biopsy

A muscle biopsy, where a small piece of muscle tissue is taken, is sometimes done to diagnose muscle disease. A hollow needle is inserted into the muscle and takes out a core of tissue. This tissue can be examined under a microscope to see if the fibers are normal.

A physical therapist uses special equipment to help teach a patient to stand and walk.

FASCINATING FACT
Muscle biopsy has been used to study muscles in athletes. Scientists have found that sprinters develop more quick-acting fibers while weight-lifters develop more slow-acting fibers.

Surgery

Most tendon tears will heal with rest and physiotherapy treatment. Severely torn tendons need to be rejoined by surgery. A badly torn Achilles tendon is a fairly common sports injury, particularly in tennis players and sprinters who use explosive bursts of muscle contraction.

Stretched tendons

Sometimes tendons become stretched, making muscle contractions ineffective. In extreme cases these tendons need surgery to shorten them.

— gastrocnemius

— Achilles tendon

— tear

FASCINATING FACT
Lifting weights was once considered to be an exercise for young men only. More and more elderly people are now doing regular weight-lifting exercises to help keep their muscles toned. Lifting weights is now a very popular form of exercise for the elderly.

A severely torn Achilles tendon must be reattached during surgery.

Taking care of the muscular system

Healthy muscles work better if they are cared for correctly. This includes being careful when exercising and providing muscles with the energy they need.

Warm up and cooling down

Warming up and cooling down when exercising is one easy way to reduce the risk of damage to muscles. Warm up by moving slowly for a few minutes. Then stretch the muscles that will be under the most strain. Carry out the reverse procedure to cool down after exercising.

A sports teacher shows students how to stretch their thigh muscles before exercise.

Massage

Massage can help keep muscles relaxed, which helps them work better. Massage is the process of rubbing muscles to make sure that they relax fully. Many athletes get regular massages to help recover from strenuous exercise.

HEALTH TIP
Strenuous activities

Strenuous activities that increase muscle strength pull very hard on tendons.

Tip: Use stretches to prevent tendon injuries.

First aid

First aid is important for quick recovery from muscular injuries. If muscles are damaged during physical activity, there is a four-step first aid procedure to follow. This is known as RICE, which stands for Rest, Ice, Compression, and Elevation. RICE can aid recovery by reducing swelling and the risk of bruising.

Rest the injured part immediately and apply ice.

In case of emergency

If you are nearby when someone is severely injured, you should:

- stay calm
- ask the injured person what hurts
- keep the injured person comfortable, but do not move them
- get medical assistance

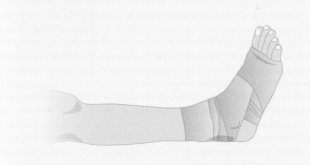

Apply compression (firm pressure), such as a bandage.

Be prepared

It is important to be prepared for emergencies. Learn emergency service numbers and practice what to ask for (police, ambulance, or fire services). In the United States, emergency services are contacted by dialing 911.

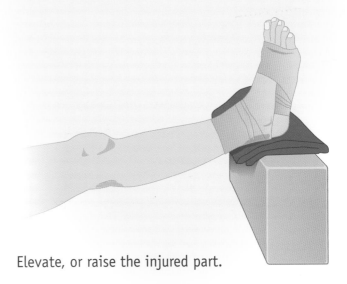

Elevate, or raise the injured part.

ACTIVITY Make a model arm

You can make a model to show how paired muscles move the arm.

What you need

- 2 rubber bands, cut to lie flat (muscles)
- 2 pieces of string, half the length of the rubber (tendons)
- 2 pieces of cardboard, three times longer than the rubber (bones)
- 1 large split pin
- hole punch
- scissors
- sticky tape

What to do

1 Overlap the two "bones" and join in the middle with the split pin.

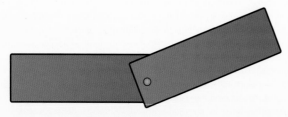

2 Punch holes in the bones, about halfway down on both sides.

3 Tie the pieces of string to one end of both rubber bands.

4 Tie the other end of the string to the hole in one bone. Tie the other end of the rubber to the hole in the other bone. Make sure the rubber bands are tight, but not over-stretched when the "arm" is straight.

5 Put sticky tape over the holes, to hold the string and rubber firm.

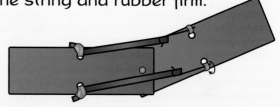

6 Move the bones like an arm bending at the elbow to see how the antagonist muscles work. One band will stretch as the other one loosens.

Glossary

abdominal	in the abdomen, the area below the chest
antagonists	muscles that work opposite each other; one relaxes as the other contracts
cells	the smallest units of living things
contract	shorten
energy	fuel for the body
filaments	very thin strands within muscle fibers that allow muscles to shorten, or contract
flexible	able to bend or move freely
limbs	arms and legs
lubricant	liquid that allows smooth movement by reducing friction
muscle fiber	long strands of muscle tissue
muscle tone	strength in the muscles that hold the body up
originate	start from
posture	the position of the body when sitting, standing, or walking
puberty	a stage when young people's bodies mature and become more adult
sheath	coating or covering of a muscle or tendon
skeletal muscles	the muscles that control body movements by moving bones
tendons	strong bands of tissue that connect muscles to bones
thigh	upper leg, above the knee
tissues	groups of similar cells that make up the fabric of body systems
torso	the trunk of the body, from the shoulders down to the buttocks
waste	unwanted products produced by the body

Index